I0424663

10 Soft Skills You Need

Mason Academy

Copyright Notice

CONTENTS

Empathy and social skills are social intelligence.
Daniel Goleman

Preface

Having the technical skills and knowledge to successfully execute your job duties is only one part of being the best you can be in the workplace. In addition to these "hard" skills, we also need "soft" skills. Soft skills are those skills which allow us to effectively work with others. No matter what your position, organization, or industry, you work with people. Taking the time to build practical soft skills can contribute to a more efficient, more harmonious, and more productive workplace, as well as to your own overall job happiness and satisfaction.

I think we all have empathy.
We may not have the courage to display it.
Maya Angelou

Chapter One

What are Soft Skills?

What are soft skills? Simply put, soft skills are the personal attributes that allow us to effectively relate to others. These skills enhance our personal interactions and lead to greater job performance and satisfaction. Unlike hard skills, which are the technical and knowledge skill set we bring to our work, soft skills are interpersonal and can be applied in a broad array of situations. Soft skills encompass both personality traits, such as optimism, and abilities which can be practiced, such as empathy. Like all skills, soft skills can be learned.

Definition of Soft Skills

Soft skills are personal attributes that allow us to effectively relate to others. Applying these skills helps us build stronger work relationships, work more productively, and maximize our career prospects. Often we place the focus of our career development efforts on hard skills – technology skills, knowledge, and other skills that specifically relate to our ability to get work-related tasks done. This means we neglect to develop our soft skills. However, soft skills are directly transferrable to any job, organization, or industry. As a result, they are an investment worth making.

Soft skills include:

- Communication
- Listening
- Showing Empathy
- Networking
- Self-confidence
- Giving and receiving feedback

Empathy and the Emotional Intelligence Quotient

Empathy is perhaps the most important soft skill we can develop for better interpersonal interactions. Empathy is the ability to identify with another person's experience. While we often think of empathy in terms only of identifying with someone's pain or negative experience, we can apply empathy in a variety of situations. Developing empathy allows us to imagine ourselves in another person's shoes, to respond to others, and even to vicariously experience others' feelings of emotions. When we demonstrate empathy, we create connections with others, which can help to build teamwork or otherwise create shared goals. Empathy also helps to forge stronger interpersonal connections between team members and colleagues, which is as important as shared goals or complementary skills when it comes to accomplishing work.

Empathy is one component of what is known as Emotional Intelligence, or EI. Emotional Intelligence is the ability to recognize and manage our feelings so that they are expressed appropriately. Exercising emotional intelligence helps to create harmonious, productive relationships. There are four key components of Emotional Intelligence:

- **Self-awareness**: The ability to recognize our own feelings and motivations
- **Self-management**: The ability to appropriately express (or not express) feelings
- **Social awareness**: Our ability to recognize the feelings and needs of others, and the norms of a given situation
- **Relationship management**: Our ability to relate effectively to others

Taken together, these skills make up our Emotional Intelligence Quotient (EQI). The EQI is a measure of your ability to exercise soft skills such as empathy.

Professionalism

The word "professionalism" often conjures up images of a cold, distant, brusque person in a nondescript navy blue suit. In fact, many people have the sense that to be "professional" is exactly the opposite of demonstrating empathy and emotional intelligence. However, professionalism is a key soft skill, and it doesn't require you to be inauthentic, distant, or detached. Professionalism is simply the ability to conduct yourself with responsibility, integrity, accountability, and excellence. Acting with professionalism also means seeking to communicate effectively with others and finding a way to be productive. Professionalism involves what may seem to be small acts, such:

- Always reporting to work on time and returning promptly from breaks
- Dressing appropriately
- Being clean and neat
- Speaking clearly and politely to colleagues, customers, and clients
- Striving to meet high standards for one's own work

Learned vs. Inborn Traits

Because soft skills are talked about as traits of a person's personality, it may seem as though you have to born with them. While some soft skills come more easily to one person than they might to another, soft skills are not inborn. Like all skills, they can be learned. Because we all have our own preferences and ways of moving through the world, some soft skills may be more difficult to learn than others. But if we think back, there are also aspects of our hard skill set that were difficult at first, though they now seem to come quite naturally to us. We develop soft skills in the same way we develop hard skills – we practice. Spending time with people who seem to be able to effortlessly demonstrate a soft skill that you find challenging is one way to build your soft skill set. Another way is to seek opportunities to practice in which the risk of failure is low, until you feel confident in your ability. You don't have to be born a networker or an empathetic person – you can learn and build these skills throughout your career.

Practical Illustration

Dee was just not a "people person." She preferred to work by herself, and her position at her company allowed her to do that most of the time. She valued her productivity and her ability to meet deadlines and exceed expectations, and anything that got in the way of that was an annoyance. When she had to interact with coworkers throughout the day, she preferred to keep the interactions as brief as possible so she could get back to work. Her coworker Angela mentioned that people often found Dee unapproachable. "I'm just not wired to be social," Dee told her. "I don't relate well to others when I feel like they're wasting my time. I've always been a loner – it just comes naturally to me." Angela explained that she also preferred to focus on her tasks and work independently, but she had learned to relate to her coworkers so that she could have a more harmonious work experience.

Angela encouraged Dee to try changing her approach to coworkers, to try to see them not as interruptions but as fellow humans who were worth paying attention to. Dee decided to try this, though it was hard for her. The next time a coworker interrupted her while she worked, Dee tried to really listen to what he needed rather than rushing him out of her office. She realized that her coworkers often didn't come to her until things were in crisis because they found her distant. She then realized that cultivating better relationships was a way to prevent crises in the workday.

The most important thing in communication
is hearing what isn't said.
Peter Drucker

Chapter Two

Communication

Communication is the most important soft skill, because all other soft skills are built on the ability to communicate clearly and professionally. Communication is more than just sending a message – it is also the ability to receive messages, listen actively, and "hear" what isn't being said. Many times we focus on learning to speak or write clearly, but this is only one component of communication – and perhaps not even the most important.

Ways We Communicate

Human communication is complex. The first thing that comes to mind when we hear the word "communication" is often words – either spoken or written. But the words we speak and hear are just one way we communicate, and some studies show that most of our communication takes place through other means.

Humans communicate in many different ways:

- **Nonverbal communication**: Communication without words, such as eye contact or posture
- **Verbal communication**: Communication with words, both written and spoken
- **Body language**: Communication through gestures, personal space, and touching
- **Artistic communication**: Communication through images and other creative media
- **Musical communication**: Communication through music, whether with lyrics or without

Most of us have a preferred method of communication, but all of use these different forms at one point or another. Learning to communicate effectively in many forms not only helps when you craft your own messages, but when you receive messages as well.

Improving Nonverbal Communication

Studies show that up to 70% of the information we communicate comes through nonverbal communication – gestures, eye contact, posture, personal space, and all the other ways we use our bodies to send messages. Other studies show that if a person's nonverbal communication and verbal communication don't match in terms of message, the listener is more likely to doubt what he or she is saying. Improving your nonverbal communication can help improve your overall ability to both send and receive messages.

Improving your nonverbal communication starts with awareness. Pay attention to how you use your body when you are talking or listening to someone. An open stance, frequent (but not continuous eye contact), nods, and a relaxed posture help to communicate that you are open and approachable, and that you are communicating honestly. A closed stance, folding your arms across your chest, staring at the floor, or refusing to make eye contact all indicate that you are not listening, or that you are not communicating openly. Shifting from foot to foot, pacing, or otherwise moving continuously indicate impatience. We do many things without thinking about them, especially when we are otherwise busy. Take time to notice both your own nonverbal communication and others', and especially your reaction to others.

Listening

The ability to receive messages is as important, if not more important, than the ability to send them. Listening is more than just hearing the words someone speaks. It is a total way of receiving verbal and nonverbal messages, processing them, and communicating that understanding back to the speaker. Many of us listen in order to respond – we are formulating our next message while another is still talking. We should instead listen to understand – to fully take in, process, and comprehend the message that is being sent.

"Active listening" is sometimes thrown around as a buzzword, but it's a valuable soft skill to develop. Active listening is a form of listening where you listen to the speaker and reflect back what you understand the speaker to have said. You may also give the speaker nonverbal feedback through nods of agreement or other techniques which indicate you are listening and understanding. Active listening involves staying focused on the present, both by giving the speaker your full attention and by keeping the discussion to the issue at hand. Reflect back to the speaker what you understand him or her to have said by carefully rephrasing the message, such as, "So, I hear you saying that…." Check for understanding and use "I" statements rather than "you" statements.

Openness and Honesty

Open, honest communication is the key to building workplace relationships and demonstrating professionalism. While you do not need to discuss personal or private topics in the workplace, being transparent and honest about work matters and generally being willing to communicate with others is vital. People can sense when someone is hiding something or withholding information, and tend not to trust him or her. This damages workplace trust and relationships, and may lead to lower productivity and morale. Each of us has a different level of comfort with what we choose to disclose about ourselves, but being willing to share parts of yourself with your colleagues also helps to build rapport.

Practical Illustration

Austin wasn't a big communicator. He liked to get right to the point so that an issue could be solved or a project moved forward. He especially didn't like it if someone seemed to be taking too long to get to the point. He tended to listen with his arms folded across his chest, and sometimes even tapped his foot without realizing it. If a person came into his office while he was working, he'd continue working while the person talked. This meant sometimes he missed important details. During his yearly review, Austin's manager told him that Austin's coworkers and direct reports felt that he never really listened, and that they were bothering him even when they had to come to him with important things. Austin's manager suggested he take a one-day communication course and try some of the techniques. Austin agreed, but only because he felt he had no choice. In the course, they talked about nonverbal communication, and Austin realized how off-putting his habits were. He decided to try to be more mindful of his nonverbal communication and listening style.

Talent wins games, but teamwork
and intelligence win championships.
Michael Jordan

Chapter Three

Teamwork

Even if you work fairly independently most of the time, inevitably you must also work with others. Finding ways to build teams that accomplish what needs to be done in the most efficient and accurate manner is often challenging, especially when bringing together team members with diverse sets of hard and soft skills. There are some basic techniques you can use when building, or working with a team to help create a cohesive unit that leverages everyone's talents and ensures that each person contributes.

Identifying Capabilities

Einstein said that everyone is a genius, but if you judge a fish by its ability to climb a tree, it will live its life thinking it is stupid. When building a team, it is key to identify the different talents, skills, and capabilities each team member brings. Identifying what each team member does well and can contribute helps ensure that work is allocated in a way that takes full advantage of the talent resources on the team. Assigning a team member work that is completely outside his or her skill set is a recipe for failure. On the other hand, leveraging all the diverse capabilities, skills, and talents on your team helps you achieve the maximum results.

When you build or join a team, take the time at the outset to ask each member what he or she brings to the team. What skills, abilities and relationships do each team member have that can enhance the project? What does each person feel he or she does well? How can the team use all these talents and capabilities to achieve the best outcome?

Get Into Your Role

When you are given a role on a team, it's important to get into it. Be sure you know what is expected of you and what you can expect of others. Even if the role is a new one or a stretch for you, it is key to step into it. This also means stepping *out* of others' roles, even if they are roles you have played before. Use your communication skills to create open, honest dialogues with your other team members so that you are all on the same page. Be clear about where your role begins and ends, and be willing to assert those boundaries. Teamwork can be challenging in the best of circumstances, but it is even more so when roles are unclear. A key step in creating a team is clearly outlining what each person's role is (and is not).

Learn the Whole Process

Knowing your role and stepping fully into it is a vital part of effective teamwork. At the same time, it's important not to get isolated in your own piece of the project. Learning the whole process not only ensures that you understand your own role and accountabilities, but helps you know what to expect of and from others. When you take the time to learn the whole process, it puts your work and your relationships with team members into a larger context. Knowing the whole process also means that you can help a colleague troubleshoot if problems arise, and that your colleagues can be of assistance should you need it. In the worst case scenario, having every member of the team knows the whole process means that others can step in if there is a crisis or breakdown in the project.

The best way to learn the whole process is to talk to team members who are working parts of a project different from your own. Take the time to ask questions and to listen actively to the answers. This not only demonstrates that you care about the outcome of the project, but that you are interested and invested in each of your teammates' work and success. Learning the whole process helps to build collaborative relationships among team members, which helps to enhance communication and overall productivity.

The Power of Flow

Psychologists define "flow" as a mental state that occurs when we are fully immersed in an activity. When we are a flow state, we are completely absorbed in what we are doing, and this produces a feeling of energized focus and enjoyment. Tapping into flow is a powerful way to increase your own productivity, and the productivity of your team. We are most likely to achieve flow when we are engaged in a task to which our skills are well matched – another reason to identify the capabilities of each person on a team. Flow also comes about more easily when we have clear goals and can focus on the process rather than the end product. Perhaps the most important key to achieving flow is to minimize interruptions when you are working.

When we can find the flow state, time seems to pass quickly without our noticing. We are also more likely to create accurate, high-quality work with fewer errors. Because we are focused totally on what we are doing, a flow state may be a key aspect of mastering a new set of skills – stretching your skill set and cultivating flow can be a great tool for professional development.

Practical Illustration

Coleen often worked as a part of a team, but preferred to focus on her part of the final product only. She communicated with her team members as needed, but didn't really understand what each of them did – it simply wasn't important to her ability to finish her part of the project. When she joined the team for a new project, the team lead, Tasha, suggested that each person describe what he or she would do on the project. Coleen didn't see the point. However, as each team member described their piece of the project and their role in the team, Coleen began to see how the project all came together – to get a larger picture. She had never thought before about what had to happen before her piece could be completed, nor what had to happen afterward. Seeing the project as a cohesive whole made her understand more clearly what the overall goal was, and knowing what each of her teammates did also helped her communicate with them more clearly.

It's not that I'm so smart, it's just that I stay with problems longer.
Albert Einstein

Chapter Four

Problem-Solving

No matter what your industry or your role, problem-solving is part of your job. Whether the problems you encounter are big or small, you solve problems every day. Learning how to apply problem-solving skills helps not only to enhance productivity, but also helps to cultivate relationships by focusing on shared goals and solutions.

Define the Problem

You can't solve a problem if you don't know what it is. The first step in solving any problem should be to define the problem itself. Oftentimes what we think is a problem is only a symptom of a larger issue. Take time to define the problem clearly, whether it's an interpersonal conflict or a hitch in a supply line. Figuring out what the problem is *exactly* and clearly defining it means you can move forward with solutions that will actually solve it, rather than just resolve the symptoms or temporarily stop the chaos. Taking time to define the problem is especially important if emotions are running high or interactions are getting heated – it puts the focus back on shared goals and allows for everyone to be heard.

Generate Alternative Solutions

Once you've defined a problem, you can move on to solutions. It is important not to just choose the first solution that presents itself. Nor should you push your own preferred solution and exclude others. Instead, take the time to generate alternative solutions. Ask the others involved what ideas they have for solving the problem. Discuss the ways in which the alternative solutions might play out, problems they might encounter, and how many obstacles can be overcome. Apply active listening and clear communication throughout. When the group has generated many solutions, discuss which one(s) you would all like to move forward with.

Evaluate the Plans

With your list of alternative solutions generated, it is time to make plans and evaluate them. Give all alternative solutions equally fair treatment. Ask the group to brainstorm potential benefits to each alternative solution or plan. Then work with the group to anticipate potential obstacles or problems with each plan. Based on these discussions, evaluate which plan or plans seem to offer the greatest benefit with the fewest drawbacks. Also consider whether the necessary resources – people, time, materials, funding – are available for each proposed plan. As the plans are evaluated, it will quickly become clear which are entirely unworkable. Narrow the list until the most workable plans are found.

Implementation and Re-Evaluation

Once the most workable plan has been chosen, it's time to implement it. It is important to communicate clearly about how the plan will be implemented, what each person's role will be, and what the goals and expected outcomes are. The other soft skills you are developing – communication and teamwork – are vital here. People must feel as though they are part of the solution if you want them to buy into it. Also provide a timeline for the plan, including the point at which the plan will be re-evaluated.

Re-evaluation of the plan is a step that often gets missed. Sometimes what appears to be the most workable plan on paper does not play out when put into action. It is important to take the time to re-evaluate the plan once it has been implemented so you can gauge how well it's working. Depending on the results, you may need to make some changes to the plan, or implement a new plan altogether. Re-evaluation helps to determine whether the original problem has, in fact, been solved.

Practical Illustration

Enrique liked to be known as the fix-it guy. He prided himself on
the ability to swoop in and resolve a crisis, and his coworkers
appreciated his ability to quickly put an end to chaos or stop a
situation from escalating. But he noticed that he seemed to put
the same fires out over and over. He could help solve a problem
in the short-term, but ultimately the same things kept coming up.
His colleague in another department, Helen, asked Enrique what
his process for solving problems was. Enrique couldn't really tell
her – he said he just looked for the most pressing need and took
care of it. Helen suggested that he get his team together and
brainstorm a list of their most common problems. They could
then identify the underlying issues, and create plans to solve
them permanently rather than just managing crises as they came
up. Enrique thought this sounded like a good idea. When they
got his team together, Enrique realized that many of the crises in
the team were caused by a lack of communication and a lack of
clear goals. He and his team brainstormed ways to create clearer,
more open communication and expectations around goals and
roles in their work. Within a few weeks, Enrique noticed that he
did not have to manage nearly as many crises.

Priority management is the answer we have to maximizing the time we have.
John C. Maxwell

Chapter Five

Time Management

We all have the same number of hours in the day, so why is it that some people seem to get so much more done? The ability to effectively manage your time is key to productivity. You may not be able to create more time in your day, but applying time management skills can help you make the most of the time you do have.

The Art of Scheduling

We know that if we want to have a meeting, get a haircut, or see our healthcare provider, we need to make an appointment. We schedule our errands and vacations. But when it comes to our own time and work we do independently, too often we take a piecemeal approach and just do whatever comes to hand first. Taking the time to schedule work tasks, even those you do independently, helps you make better use of your time. Instead of doing work as it comes to you, take the time to slot in a block of time on your schedule for each task. Don't forget to schedule in breaks, too. Scheduling tasks make them a priority – after all, you wouldn't just skip a doctor's appointment or other scheduled obligation. Seeing something on your schedule also helps you remember that it needs to get done. Scheduling can take some time to master – you may discover that tasks take much more (or much less) time than you plan for. Spend a week or so keeping track of how you spend your work time so that you can better plan ahead for how much time to schedule a given task or project.

Prioritizing

Managing your priorities is important in managing your time. Taking the time to determine what is most important, whether in terms of value or in terms of completion, is the first step. Take time each week to determine what your priorities for the coming days are. Slot these into your schedule first. This allows you to ensure that time is blocked off and resources allocated for the most important tasks and projects. When we don't take time to set priorities, everything becomes equally urgent. This means that we move from task to task in a way that is haphazard and does not make the best use of our time or energy. Setting priorities helps ensure that you take care of the things that are most pressing or which deliver the most value. Prioritizing is especially vital when working with others. If people who must work together have different senses of what the priorities are, this can lead to miscommunication, conflict, and reduced productivity.

Managing Distractions

A major key to productivity, especially if you want to find a flow state, is to manage your distractions. Distractions happen; we can minimize them and manage them, but never eliminate them altogether. Creating a plan for managing distractions is an important time management skill. The first step is to determine what your major distractions are. Is it colleagues popping into your office? Is it your email or voicemail? Do you get bored with routine tasks if you have to focus on them too long? Figuring out what your major distractions are can help you brainstorm solutions and better manage them.

Some common distractions are:

- Colleagues stopping by to chat
- Checking email or voicemail
- Noise in the environment
- Clutter in your workspace
- Boredom after spending too long on one task

You can solve these by:

- Establishing "open door" hours
- Closing your door or otherwise indicating "Please Do Not Disturb"
- Using noise canceling headphones
- Setting a regular time to check voicemail and email
- Letting calls go to voicemail
- De-cluttering your workspace
- Building in breaks

The Multitasking Myth

Multitasking is exactly what it sounds like – trying to do more than one thing at a time. Many of us multitask throughout our day – listening to a colleague while checking email, working on a document while talking on the phone. We have the idea that we get more done when we multitask or that this is the best way to maximize our time. However, studies show that 30-40% more time is spent when you multitask rather than when you mono-task (work on one thing at a time). Multitasking also means your attention is divided, which can lead to miscommunication and errors. Multitasking can also damage relationships, as it may convey that we are not really interested in what another is saying. It can be difficult to break the multitasking habit, but it is important if we are the best we can be

Practical Illustration

Cliff was one of the busiest people in the office. He always had at least three things going on. To make the most of his time, he did two or more things at once – edited a document on the screen while he was on a conference call, filed papers while he talked to one of his direct reports. He just could never get ahead – it seemed the harder he worked, the more behind he fell. He didn't understand why his office mate, Shawna, always seemed to be so on top of things. She only ever worked on one thing at a time. She let her calls roll to voicemail, and only checked her email four times a day. Cliff didn't understand how she could possibly get everything done that she did. She also seemed so much less harried than he did – she even had time to take a little break a couple of times a day to walk around and get a cup of tea. He asked her what her secret was. "I only do one thing at a time," she said. "This way my full attention is on one thing, and then I can move on to another later." She told him to try it for one week. He scoffed, but agreed since he was so stressed. To his amazement, Cliff found that tasks took less time than he thought they would, and he was able to work much more efficiently when he focused on one thing at a time.

Weakness of attitude becomes weakness of character.
Albert Einstein

Chapter Six

Attitude and Work Ethic

Creating a positive attitude is one of the best things you can do for your productivity and your workplace happiness. People who have a consistently positive attitude are seen as approachable and can build more effective workplace relationships. A positive attitude also serves you well when you face challenges or setbacks – it breeds resilience. Coupled with a positive attitude, a strong work ethic helps you build strong relationships with teammates and superiors. A solid work ethic also helps you find reward in the work you do, and shows a dedication not just to goals and outcomes but to your overall professional development.

What Are You Working For?

Being clear about what you're working for is an important part of building a positive attitude and strong work ethic. If you are not sure what you are working for, it can be difficult or even impossible to fully invest in a project or in developing your skills. Take time to clarify what your personal goals are, both in terms of specific projects and in terms of your overall career. Set specific goals and then create plans to achieve them. Tie these goals to your day to day tasks and responsibilities so that you can keep them in sight. When working with a team, it is also vital that you outline clear group goals. Know what each member of the group is working for, and what the group is collectively working for. Find ways to consistently tie individual tasks or steps to the overarching group goals and to individual members' personal goals.

Caring for Others vs Caring for Self

Is there really a difference between caring for others and caring for yourself? Too often, we assume that to show care and concern for others and their needs, we have to put ourselves and our needs at the bottom of the list. We may believe that we can either practice self-care or be a good colleague and team member who demonstrates compassion for others, but that we cannot be both. However, when we come to the realization that we have shared goals with those we work with, we can find a way to both care for ourselves and care for others. We may also realize that caring for ourselves is in itself a way of demonstrating care for others, that by taking good care of ourselves, we become the best colleague we can be, which demonstrates care for others.

Even more, we may hold the false belief that there can only be one "winner" in any given situation. As a result, we may believe that we can pursue our own goals or help others pursue theirs, but never do both. Seeing the ways in which everyone is interconnected, and the way in which everyone's success benefits the entire group is an important attitude shift. When we can find a way to care for others and ourselves, we develop a more positive, productive workplace.

Building Trust

Nothing undermines productivity and morale in a workplace like lack of trust. If people don't trust you, they find it hard to work with you, invest in you, or pursue shared goals. Take the time to build trust with those you work with, and everyone will thrive. Many of the soft skills help to build trust – effective communication, openness and honesty, a positive attitude and a strong work ethic. Demonstrating that you are trustworthy helps not only to build personal relationships, but also to create buy-in for your initiatives and projects. People who are deemed trustworthy by colleagues share some characteristics:

- They are skilled at their jobs
- They are passionate about their work , with a strong work ethic
- They communicate honestly and value transparency
- They have others' best interests at heart
- They care about people and demonstrate this
- They are self-aware

Work Is Its Own Reward

One result of adopting a positive attitude and strong work ethic is that you begin to see work as its own reward. When we operate from this standpoint, we are no longer working with others or completing tasks based on what we will gain financially or professionally from doing so, and this makes us seem more engaged and trustworthy. There is nothing wrong with valuing our salaries and other compensation as they are a vital part of why we work. However, when we take the focus off the material rewards for work and instead focus on the satisfaction we derive from the work itself, we are better able to grow and thrive.

A person who clearly loves what they do and considers it a reward in itself is also more trustworthy, as others do not question his or her motives. If it is difficult for you to consider your work as anything other than the source of a paycheck or path to advancement, it may be time for you to consider why you do the work you do. Learning to practice gratitude around your work is one way to learn to see it as its own reward. What does your work provide you in terms of satisfaction, contentment, excitement, and other nonmaterial benefits? Are you excited to do the work you do? Why or why not? Do you feel content at the end of the day with what you've accomplished? Every day won't be a dream come true but if you can find a way to love the work you do the majority of the time, you are on the path to greater professional and personal happiness.

Practical Illustration

Yuki always said she was only in her job for the paycheck. She really wanted to pay off her student loans and credit card debt, and she worked as many hours as she could to earn the money she needed. She was good at her job and completed her tasks accurately and on time, but seemed to derive little pleasure from it. She worked hard all week and counted the days until Friday. She often seemed unhappy or bored with the work. Her manager asked her what she felt she was working for – what were her goals? Yuki explained that she was working for a paycheck. Her manager then asked what she would be working for when the debt was gone. Yuki couldn't answer. Her manager suggested she think more broadly about what she was working for, and how she could find other rewards in her work. They brainstormed a list of Yuki's professional and personal goals and then discussed how Yuki could view her work in the context of these goals. Yuki began to feel more engaged in her work.

You must always be able to predict what's next
and have the flexibility to evolve.
Marc Benioff

Chapter Seven

Adaptability

Two of the most important skills you can have are adaptability and flexibility. Some people mistakenly think that the ability to change according to the needs of a situation or a willingness to compromise shows the weakness of a lack of conviction. In reality, the ability to compromise, adapt to change and still thrive is key to success in the fast-paced workplaces most of us find ourselves in. Change can be scary, but learning to adapt and flex as needed is an investment worth making.

Getting Over the Good Old Days Syndrome

"But that's how we've always done it."

"Things were better back when we….."

Do you find yourself saying these things? Most of us fall prey to the "good old days" syndrome, where we look back at the past and believe that everything was better. This can pose a serious obstacle to our ability to adapt to change. If we are convinced that the good old days were best, we are unlikely to give a new way of doing things a fair try. When you find yourself thinking back to the good old days, give yourself a reality check. Ask yourself if things were really as good as you think you remember. Most of us romanticize the past. Be honest with yourself. Try to recall obstacles, problems, or difficulties you had with the thing you remember as so good.

Changing to Manage Process

One of the most common situations in which we will need to change, flex, and adapt is when processes change. In order to navigate the new process, and help others to do the same, we need to change not only what we do but how we approach it. New technology, globalizing businesses, and changing needs all lead to changes in our work processes. If we hold on to the old way of doing things, we risk reduced productivity (and revenue), as well as conflict and other challenges. When we adapt to a new process, we are not just learning a new way of doing a specific task, we are demonstrating our ability to adapt to changing circumstances, learn new skills, and work with others.

Changing to Manage People

Managing people is not a one-size-fits-all ability. People need different things from a manager. Some need lots of feedback and guidance. Others prefer to work independently most of the time and to get feedback only at regularly scheduled intervals. Some people need a great deal of hands-on training with technology or equipment, while others will come into your organization as experts. Taking the time to learn what your people need, and then changing your management style to meet those needs, is hugely important to workplace success. When you adapt your management style to meet the specific needs of the people you manage, this demonstrates that you care for others, that rather than expecting them to conform to your preferred way of doing things, you want to invest in them and help them grow. Take the time to ask the people you manage what they need from you, what their goals are, and how you can be a better manager, supervisor and colleague. Then take steps to make the changes that you feel will be most helpful.

Showing You Are Worth Your Weight in Adaptability

How can you showcase your adaptability at work? Studies show that people who are highly adaptable may be more highly valued at work than those who are highly skilled but less willing to adapt, flex, and change. Take the time to show how adaptable you are, and your workplace is likely to see you as a worthwhile investment.

Some ways to demonstrate adaptability on the job are:

- Be open to alternative solutions when your first suggestion does not go over well or succeed
- Be willing to take on new roles, even when they are a stretch for your skills
- Be willing to help others generate alternative solutions or plans
- Be willing to accept the unexpected
- Keep your calm, even when things are moving fast or are stressful
- Demonstrate confidence in your ability to complete the job even when you've had to adapt or flex

Practical Illustration

Martin had been a manager for more than 30 years. He had developed a tough but fair style that he applied impartially to all his direct reports. He thought it was best to treat everyone the same – that way things were fair and everyone knew what to expect. When he started at his new organization, he noticed that many of his new direct reports seemed to need a lot of handholding. This was frustrating for Martin. He didn't understand why they couldn't just do the work as assigned. Mistakes were common, too.

One day when talking with a manager in another division, Martin expressed his frustration. "Sometimes our younger employees need a little more guidance," he said. "They are newly out of college and aren't sure what to do. They are used to having a lot of face time with their supervisors. Maybe you could try that and see if it works." Martin didn't want to have to change, but he also didn't want things to continue as they were. He tried spending one on one time with his new direct reports each time he assigned them new work, so that they could discuss goals and expectations. He quickly noticed that the work improved.

Self-confidence is the first requisite to great undertakings.
Samuel Johnson

Chapter Eight

Self-Confidence

The single greatest thing you can do for your own success is develop and learn how to show self-confidence. Self-confidence is not egotistic or acting like you're better than others. Self-confidence is simply the belief that you know what to do and how to do it, that you are good at what you do and that you can handle whatever comes your way. Demonstrating self-confidence helps to engender trust in you, and demonstrates that you are skilled and adaptable.

Confident Traits

What does it mean to be confident? Studies show that confident people share many of the same traits, even across cultures and industries. Cultivating those traits you already have, and developing those that you do not yet have, will build your overall self-confidence. Remember; self-confidence is about building yourself up, not tearing others down. When you're confident, you make others around you feel confident too.

Some common traits of confident people include:

- They are not afraid to be wrong
- They are willing to take a stand, even if they end up being wrong
- They value finding out what is right more than they value being right
- They listen more than they speak
- They do not seek the spotlight, and they share the spotlight with others
- They ask for help when they need it
- They think in possibilities, not obstacles – they ask "Why not?"
- They don't put others down
- They aren't afraid to look silly or foolish
- They acknowledge their mistakes
- They seek feedback from only those who matter
- They accept compliments
- They "walk their talk"

Self-Questionnaire

How confident are you? It can be hard to assess our own self-confidence. Taking some time to ask a few questions and answer them honestly can help you gauge the areas where your confidence is high and the areas in which you can develop greater self-confidence. Ask yourself if you agree with these statements:

- I intuitively know what's right for me
- I walk my talk
- I am honest with others
- I am honest with myself
- I feel comfortable being wrong
- I am more interested in finding out what is right than being right
- It is not important to me that I be right all the time
- I feel like I can meet any challenge
- I operate well under pressure
- I do not put others down
- I like to share the spotlight with others
- I have a clear vision for my life

Surefire Self-Confidence Building Tactics

Self-confidence is a trait that can be built. In fact, a few very simple tactics can help you quickly build your self-confidence. As you become more confident, you will have experiences that will build your confidence even more. Here are ten sure-fire tips for building self-confidence:

- **Dress your best!** Knowing you look good is a key to feeling good about yourself. When you know you look good, you project confidence. Take the time to choose clothes that fit well and which you feel good in. A good haircut that is easy for you to style is also important. If you enjoy make-up, jewelry, or other types of adornment, find pieces you love and that make you feel great.

- **Stand up straight!** Good posture is a quick, free way to build your confidence. Stand up straight and keep your shoulders back. Don't be afraid to take up space. A bonus of good posture is that you breathe more deeply and get more oxygen, which may mean you have more focus.

- **Practice gratitude!** When you take the time each day to practice gratitude, you see how many blessings you have in your life. This builds your confidence and appreciation for your life.

- **Compliment others!** Confident people take the time to compliment others. When you compliment others, you project that you have concern and appreciation for others.

- **Accept compliments!** When someone compliments you, accept it. Too often we say "Yes, but..." instead of just saying "Thank you."

- **Spend time with people who build you up**. This helps to keep you focused on the positive.

Build Up Others

One key trait of people who have high self-confidence is that they build up others rather than tearing them down. Having self-confidence means that you do not feel competitive with others, their success doesn't take away from your own. Find ways to build up others. Compliment others. Acknowledge their contributions and express your gratitude. Being a mentor can also help to build others up by helping them develop skills, which will help them develop their own self-confident

Practical Illustration

"Mark Twain was so good with crowds that he became, in competition with singers and dancers and actors and acrobats, one of the most popular performers of his time. It is so unusual, and so psychologically unlikely, too, for a great writer to be a great performer, too.... " -*Kurt Vonnegut*

I like criticism. It makes you strong.

LeBron James

Chapter Nine

Ability to Learn

No one likes criticism, but the ability to learn from it is important to professional and personal development. Learning to accept and learn from criticism is a valuable investment in you. The ability to listen to and accept criticism is a key component of self-confidence. It also demonstrates that you value what others have to say, and helps develop a sense that you are committed to what you do and to your own growth.

Wow, You Mean I'm Not Perfect?

It can come as a shock when we get feedback that we're not as perfect as we might like to think. However, one of the hallmarks of a confident person is the willingness to recognize mistakes and accept that sometimes we are wrong. The key is to keep the focus on improvement, not on defending ourselves or on the reasons why we did the thing we are being criticized for. When you accept that you're not perfect, you will have gained a valuable skill. Remember that no one expects you to be perfect; they just expect you to be the best you can. And criticism is offered in the spirit of helping you achieve excellence, not to make you feel bad.

Listen with an Open Mind

Your active listening skills come in very handy when you're learning to accept and learn from criticism. It is tempting to defend ourselves when we receive criticism, but it is vital to resist this. When someone offers you feedback or criticism, listen with an open mind. You may not agree with all (or any) of what he or she has to say, but it is important to hear the person out. Reflect back what you understand the person to have said, and check for understanding. Answer any questions non-defensively, and do not interrupt. Listen to understand, not to respond.

Analyze and Learn

After someone has given you feedback or criticism, it is fine to ask for time to consider what he or she has said. Always thank the person for the feedback. Take time to analyze the feedback and decide what items you want to act on. Give yourself time, especially if you feel defensive. Even if you do not agree with everything the person said, see what you can draw out of the feedback that you can learn from. When you have analyzed the feedback, choose some action items that you can use going forward. You should then investigate training, mentoring, or other ways in which you can improve on in the areas of feedback that you think are valid. If you have difficulty analyzing the feedback, seek out the help of a supervisor or trusted colleague.

Clear the Air and Don't Hold Any Grudges

Even when it's not meant to be, criticism and feedback can feel extremely personal. When someone gives you feedback, it's important to clear the air and not hold onto any bad feelings or grudges. Take the time to thank the person for his or her time, and for caring enough to give you feedback. Affirm the relationship, especially if the criticism has been harsh or difficult to hear. Remember that when people give you feedback, they are doing so with your best interests at heart. If you find yourself feeling defensive or holding on to negative feelings even after the feedback session, make sure to find a way to clear the air as soon as possible. This demonstrates not only that you are committed to your own growth, but that you value the relationship with the person who gave you the feedback.

Practical Illustration

Everyone dreaded having to give Delia feedback. She never wanted to hear that she had done anything less than perfect – she always had a reason for why she had taken the actions she had. If someone gave her criticism, she would be frosty for several days and not want to talk to them. She seldom acted on feedback unless she got it from her manager. Delia didn't understand why it seemed like people were attacking her and wondered if this was why she was not being promoted. Her manager suggested that Delia try learning new skills around feedback. She took a weekend course and realized that she had not been listening with an open mind, and had been damaging her relationships with her coworkers. She decided to try some of the techniques she learned so she could learn from others' feedback.

Networking is an essential part of building wealth.
Armstrong Williams

Chapter Ten

Networking

Networking is more than just a buzzword. Taking the time to network and build relationships is an important soft skill. Networking helps you create connections with others, which expands your circle of learning and support. Networking is more than meeting people or connecting with them on the Internet. It involves building mutually beneficial links where you can learn from and benefit from each other and the relationship.

Redefine Need

When many people think of networking, they think of it terms of what they need or what they can get from the networking relationship. Networking can be more beneficial if we instead think of what we can give in our networking relationships. Think about what you have to offer people instead only of what you need from them. When you think in terms of what you can offer as well as what you need from others, it expands your network. You begin to seek out people to whom you can offer yourself, your expertise, and talents rather than just those who have something to offer you. Seeing yourself as someone with much to offer also helps to boost your self-confidence.

Identifying Others' Interests

When you network with others, it's crucial to identify others' interests. This helps you identify common interests and goals, as well as areas in which you can offer of yourself. When you meet a new person, ask about his or her goals and interests. Ask yourself how they mesh with your own goals and interests. How do they line up with the goals and interests of your organization? How can you integrate your interests with others' to find common ground? What common goals do you have? What can you offer of yourself to help others reach their goals? How can they help you reach your goals? Focusing on ways in which your goals and interests integrate with others' helps create a strong, powerful network that goes beyond simple friendship.

Reach Out

To be able to network, you have to reach out. There are many
ways to do this, both online and in person. One of the easiest
ways to reach out is to join professional social networking sites
such as LinkedIn, and look for people in your industry or who
share your interest. Join groups, both online and in person –
professional groups and associations, groups which promote
skills you want to develop (such as Toastmasters) and groups
that work for causes you value are all good choices. No matter
what you choose as a method of meeting people, the important
part of networking is to talk to people. Approach people and start
a conversation, and cultivate a presence that makes you
approachable. Be responsive when people contact you via email
or phone. Make time in your schedule each week to work on
networking – schedule it as you would any other important task.
Use your soft skills – listening actively, projecting self-
confidence, build others up, as you network.

When to Back Off

As important as knowing how and when to reach out is knowing
when to back off. If it becomes clear that the person you are
trying to connect with is not responding, it is time to move on.
The last thing you want is for someone to feel pursued. Be
willing to back off if a person appears to be trying to distance
him or herself. Also, be aware of being too self-promoting, this
can be off-putting. Know that you have much to offer to others
and that someone not wanting to build a networking relationship
with you is not a reflection of your worth as a person.

Practical Illustration

Gwen's manager suggested she join a professional social networking site. She thought it would help Gwen as she stepped into her new role with more responsibility if she networked with people in similar positions. Gwen wasn't sure – she wasn't even sure how to create a profile or use the site. She spent some time with her coworker Kwame, who managed the social media for their company. Kwame helped Gwen choose a professional looking headshot for her profile. Then they entered in her information, focusing on her education, work history, and her current role. Kwame advised her to keep her presence on the site professional and positive. They then sought out groups on the site. Gwen joined a group for professional women, a group for people in roles like hers, and a group for alumni of her university. He helped her craft personal, friendly messages to people who seemed to have the same goals and interests. Within a week or so, Gwen had made contact with several people who were very experienced in roles like hers, and who had advice to give. She was also able to help some new alumni from her university with advice on their job searches.

Skill to do comes of doing.
Ralph Waldo Emerson

Closing Thoughts

- **Daniel Tammet**: I consider social skill a bit like learning a language. I've been practicing it for so long over so many years. I've almost lost my accent.

- **Lindsay Fox**: Personal relationships are always the key to good business. You can buy networking; you can't buy friendships.

- **Bryant H**. **McGill**: One of the most sincere forms of respect is actually listening to what another has to say.

- **Jane Goodall**: Change happens by listening.

www.ingramcontent.com/pod-product-compliance
Lightning Source LLC
Chambersburg PA
CBHW020329290526
45785CB00007B/2979